GT

A WORKABLE BELIEF

A Workable Belief

THOUGHTS ON
THE APOSTLES' CREED

Gilleasbuig Macmillan

Series Editor: *Duncan B Forrester*

SAINT ANDREW PRESS
EDINBURGH

First published in 1993 by
SAINT ANDREW PRESS
121 George Street, Edinburgh EH2 4YN

Copyright © Gilleasbuig Macmillan 1993

ISBN 0 7152 0683 4

British Library Cataloguing in Publication Data

A catalogue record for this book
is available from the British Library.

ISBN 0715206834

Cover photograph by *Paul Turner.*

Cover design by *Mark Blackadder.*

Printed and bound by Bell and Bain Ltd, Glasgow.

Contents

Editor's Introduction

ALL down the ages Christians have reflected on their faith and its bearing on life. These reflections have taken a great variety of forms, but one of the most common has been the sermon. For generations notable preachers were well-known public figures, and books of sermons were a well-known literary genre. In many places people queued to hear great preachers, whose sermons were reported in the press, and discussed and dissected afterwards. Sermons launched great movements of mission, and revival, and social change. Sometimes influential preachers were imprisoned by the authorities so that their disturbing challenge should not be heard.

Nowhere was this tradition more lively than in Scotland. But today, some people say, the glory has departed. If you want to find great preaching today, the critics say, go to Africa, or Latin America, or to Black churches in the States. No longer in Scotland do people pack in their hundreds into huge churches to hear great preachers. The sermon seems to have lost its centrality in Scottish life. The conviction and the emotional surcharge that once sustained a great succession of notable preachers seems hard to find today. Has secularisation destroyed the appetite for sermons? Has the modern questioning of authority eroded the preaching office? Do Christians no longer reflect on their faith, or do they do it in other and newer ways?

This series of books shows that the tradition of preaching is still very much alive and well. It has changed, it is true, and it has adapted to new circumstances and new challenges. It is not the same as it was in the long afterglow of the Victorian pulpit. Reflection by the Scots on their faith, as these books illustrate, is perhaps more varied than it was in the past, and their sermons are briefer. But Scottish preaching is still passionate, thoughtful, biblical, challenging, and deeply concerned with the relevance of the gospel to the needs of today's world.

The reflections on the Christian faith in these books are challenging, disturbing, nourishing. They proclaim a Word that is alive and active, and penetrates to the depths of things, a Word that speaks of hope and worth, of forgiveness and new beginnings, of justice, peace and love. And so they invite the reader to engage afresh with the everlasting gospel.

Duncan B Forrester

Foreword

THIS book contains short talks prepared for Sunday Morning Communion in St Giles' Cathedral, Edinburgh. Although I hope they will be read by people who were not present when they were delivered, readers may find it useful to imagine the context, of both sight and sound, in which their hearers heard them. A church service is an amalgamation of many things. It is not fanciful to claim that in the old days Sunday worship began with Saturday's preparation—brushing your boots, peeling the potatoes—and even today there will be some link between how you come to church and what you do when you get there. The pictures in the windows, the organ music, the candles lit, the white cloth on the Holy Table, the cross carried before the choir in procession, the sight of people familiar and visiting, all help to do far more than set the stage for worship, for they remain with you through-out the service. Religion is the inhabiting of an environment of nourishing imagery more than the holding of opinions.

Worshippers may reasonably expect to find certain ingredients in a Sunday service, but not all of these elements need be in the sermon. The more the opportunity for thanksgiving, penitence, concern for others, the assurance of forgiveness, the recollection of the heart of Christian belief, and the reading of the Bible are included in the service, the less these things will require to be incorporated specifically in the sermon. I even suspect that some of the best sermons may be given in services which would have been perfectly good and complete services without a sermon at all. That must be even more the case when the service is Holy

Communion. As with many things, preaching may achieve most when it is done in awareness of its possibilities as realistically modest.

It has been my good fortune over these twenty years to have around me as I try to preach not only the sturdy pillars of an ancient church, but the music of skilled singers and organists, and the company of a good mixture of people for whose generous tolerance I have much cause to be thankful.

Gilleasbuig Macmillan
APRIL 1993

Publishers Note

The publisher would like to acknowledge kind permission to use extracts from the poems 'Transfiguration' (pages 48-49) and 'The Church' (pages 58-60) from Edwin Muir's: *The Collection,* co-published by Faber & Faber 1963, London and Oxford University Press, New York.

The quotation from Frederick Buechner (pages 56-57) comes from the book *Wishful Thinking: A Theological ABC.*

1

Posts in the Snow

WHEN snow falls on the narrow road which runs where horses once pulled carts along the side of the hill, around the rocks, zigzagging to the crest, the tracks are quickly covered, and the modest highway seems to have been removed and the hill restored to its former state in shimmering radiant glory. On such a road they fix tall posts, some on one side of the road, some on the other, in an arrangement which informs the practised driver of the location of the hidden road. Sometimes you drive to the right of the post, sometimes to the left (and if you are not familiar with the custom of having such posts, you can sometimes go on the wrong side of them).

It seems to me that the usefulness to Christian people of the Apostles' Creed (and other creeds and other things as well, but the Apostles' Creed is my subject now) is comparable to the usefulness of these big wooden posts to travellers in the snow. We hear faith described as a journey or pilgrimage, Christ as the Way. It is easy to develop the idea and identify signposts, ditches, crossroads, traffic lights. I merely add snow posts to the list. The post is not the road. Neither the post nor the road is the journey. The journey is not the traveller. The various stages or themes of the Creed are not themselves the living of Christian faith, but indicators of where the journey of faith is likely to be found, though you have to use your head, and sometimes it is not clear which side of the post it is better to take.

When I say the Creed is like the snow posts in that it is not

1

the road, or the journey, I am not at all trying to put the Creed down or diminish its value. Much the same might be said of the Bible. The ancient Old Testament prohibition of idols has only trivial relevance to us if it is confined to a rejection of the worship of metal or stone statues; but it has deep and wide significance for us when we see it as asserting that apart from God nothing is to be worshipped—not ideas, not customs, not words, not creeds, not books, not even THE book. (The distinguished Methodist minister Donald Soper said some years ago that the Bible is a magnificent servant, but an intolerable master. Exactly.) To treat the Creed as if it were above comment, criticism, re-interpretation is to fossilise it, or idolise it—and certainly to rob it of its great usefulness. I know it may seem that the Creed is a summary of those central things which Christian people believe, and by that understanding of it we could easily see the beliefs as central, our lives and conduct as a failed half-following of its implications. But that is to regard 'believing' as something like 'thinking' or 'holding such-and-such things to be true'. Christian believing is much more practical than that. 'I believe in God' does not mean 'I think there is a God', but 'I trust in God', and that is more a matter of wide practical disposition and behaviour than a matter of holding opinions.

It is no accident that the Creed contains the things it does. We might have written it differently. It reflects the time in which it was drawn up, and the controversies and insights of that period. We may find elements in it difficult to understand or hard to swallow. One thing I beg you not to do—to reject any part of it before you have considered more than one way of interpreting it. I would indeed say much the same about not *affirming* the Creed without realising that there is more than one way of understanding or interpreting any part of it. Simplistic affirmation and simplistic rejection of religious claims have that obvious factor in common.

2

There is a sort of religious zeal which has this important thing in common with a sort of hostility to religion—they each seem to say that the answers to questions about religion are clear, and there is no mystery or vagueness about the matter. Both are far removed from the approach which holds that our efforts at defining religious truth are never precise, that the heart of the matter is swathed in great mystery, that none of our statements of doctrine ever tells the whole story. We should therefore not be intimidated by statements from the past, or regard them as liable to suffocate free thought or freeze our own contemporary attempts to say what the Faith is. We should treat them with the honour and respect due to expressions which have stood the test of centuries and carried the acceptance of the Christian community, and our challenge should be not to jettison them when they fail to fit our patterns of thought, but to produce our own responses to the great things of Christ, permitting ancient and new to work together upon the imaginations of any who wish to consider an old religion claiming to be capable of renewal.

I have chosen the title *A Workable Belief* because I wish to present the Apostles' Creed in a way which emphasises its practical value. The word 'creed' may have come to bear unattractive associations, rather like the word 'theological', suggesting pointless preoccupation with unnecessary and divisive details, trying to answer questions which nobody is asking and then battering people for getting the answers wrong. The old Scottish custom of calling the Creed 'The Belief' has much to be said for it, not least because many people may not know that the word 'Creed' is merely an English form of the Creed's first word in Latin—*credo* which means 'I believe'. When I say that the Creed is practical, I am not suggesting that you can bring problems of personal or social morality to it and 'read' the answers out of it as if you were reading a table converting Fahrenheit temperatures to

3

Celsius. What I am suggesting is that believing is not so much about holding religious opinions as about how the basic ingredients of religion affect every area of our lives. Most of all I mean that worship is not an entry into a special and 'religious' world, but a means of putting the one real world into a good and useful perspective; and since the themes of the Creed coincide so largely with the ingredients of Christian worship, it will not be surprising when these themes serve the purpose of worship in setting daily life in a great context of trust and hope.

2

I believe

IT was a perfectly reasonable point that was made to me after a Sunday morning service. It suggested that the sermon which I had given went in one direction, while the Creed which followed the sermon went in the opposite direction, at least in its opening word, the word 'I'. The sermon spoke of the sharing of belief, some aspects being held more strongly by some people and others by other people, and of how a balanced faith is held not by individuals but by the Church. The questioner accepted that, but asked how I could proceed immediately to begin the Creed with the words '*I* believe'. (The longer Nicene Creed began in the plural, 'We believe', and though in the Western Churches—Catholic and Protestant—it was later changed to 'I believe', the Orthodox Churches of Eastern Europe have continued to say 'We believe'. The old plural is also being restored among Churches throughout the world).

You may, of course, interpret the words 'I believe' to mean 'I, inasmuch as I am a member of the Church, and not merely as an expression of personal opinion, believe'—or 'The Church believes, and I go along with it as far as I can'. You may also regard the act of saying the Creed together in a church service as a corporate act which modifies the element of private or individual judgment or commitment. Presumably that is what we do when we sing hymns, where it is surely not expected that every person singing them is giving expression to wholehearted agreement with the thoughts, feelings or commitments which appear to have been in the minds of the hymn-writers. (Otherwise it would be more than strange for a person who feels sceptical about much of the Creed to be heard singing 'Jesus my Shepherd, Husband, Friend, my Prophet, Priest and King'). It would, however, be too easy simply to say 'Treat the Creed as if it were a hymn', though the similarities are worth contemplating.

Even if we accept that the saying of the Creed is properly a communal act (even if you are saying it alone in an empty chapel, on a hillside, or in bed) there must be kept a place for 'I'. However important it is to emphasise the corporate basis of belief, the individual element remains. We are not required to choose between restricting our claims of belief to those permitted by our private judgment, and swallowing, lock, stock and barrel, the official pronouncements of Church authorities. The former would lead us to drink from very shallow pools. The latter would leave us little better than spokes in a prayer wheel. The happier situation is more like a dialogue, or perhaps a see-saw, where individual judgment and common inheritance are in conversation with each other, and modification of either side is possible. (I have a picture in my head of a delicately balanced see-saw, with a seagull walking to and fro along the plank, which dips under the gull's weight, now on one side, now on the other. Is faith, or the believing Church member, a bit like that seagull, with the two ends of the plank representing individual thought and the shared tradition of the Church?)

Believing is much more than making judgments or holding opinions. There is a huge distinction between *believing that* and *believing in*, and in the Creed we talk of believing in. The most important difference between *that* and *in* where belief is concerned is that you believe that certain things are true or right, but you believe in people. You believe that The White House, Washington DC is the residence of the President of the United

6

States of America, and you believe that irrespective of what your attitude to any particular current president may be; but to say you believe in the President means that you trust him. If you are ill your doctor may give you plenty information about your illness, its likely development, and the likely consequences of certain forms of treatment. You may believe that everything the doctor tells you is true. But you go much further than accepting the accuracy of the information when you say 'I believe in the doctor'. Then you are saying you trust the doctor to have your best interest at heart, and to regard you with both the professional and the personal qualities which you wish to find in whoever is your doctor. There is possibly no more common, or more basic misunderstanding in relation to Christian belief, and to the Creeds in particular, than the confusing of these two sorts of belief, and the supposing that the Creed begins with an expression of opinion about matters of fact, when in reality it begins with an expression of personal trust, of the sort we feel about someone on whom we know we can rely.

Let me try to say three things about the sort of personal trust that is involved in our saying 'I believe in … ' when we say the Creed. It is not one in a series of trusts, as if we were to say that we believe in the doctor, the gardener, the travel agent, the weather forecaster, and God. It is more like a background trust underlying, but not entirely separate from, the more specific instances of trust in people. Religious trust is what you might call 'focus trust' which helps us see our specific commitments and detachments in focus, and reminds us of our place in the world, each of us important and profoundly significant, but not the centre of things.

The second thing is that the description or definition which I have given of religious trust is also the description or definition I would give of worship. Worship and believing are not two distinct elements in Christian life. The notion, though probably quite widely held, that first you have 'beliefs' and secondly you bring your beliefs to church and use them in worship, seems to me to be an unfortunate and unnecessary segmentation of something much more whole and united. Many definitions may be given of church services, and of the other acts which could come within a broad definition of Christian worship. All of them, however, should leave room for an understanding which holds believing and worshipping to be so very close to each other that they become virtually interchangeable words. They refer to a re-orientation of the individual within a large perspective of providence and grace and hope, the chief signs and imagery of these benefits being the life, spirit and impact of Jesus Christ.

When we ask for more information about the nature of the basic personal focus-trust which is the heart of believing and of worship, one answer is that the entire Creed, and nothing less, provides a sort of sketch of the ground and object of our trust. We cannot seek to extract from the word 'God' all that informs a Christian understanding of Creator, but rather go on to see how Christ gives us our awareness of creation as of forgiveness. That is the third thing I wish to say about 'I believe in ...'. The Creed speaks of a trust that offers a relationship to the heart of all that is. Instead of getting bogged down by our inability to imagine God (for imagining God has never been part of either Jewish or Christian religion) we do better to see how the breadth and depth of fundamental trusting are focussed and facilitated in Jesus the Christ.

3

God the Father Almighty

Lord of all being, throned afar,
Thy glory flames from sun and star:
Centre and soul of every sphere,
Yet to each loving heart how near.

WHEN we try to speak of God, there is much to be said for calling to our aid poets and musicians. For one thing, they know they are not so much giving definitions as offering pictures, metaphors, imagery through which something of The Mystery may be suggested, though never confined. There is much danger in our use of the word 'God'. We tend to think that it is not at all metaphorical. We know that a reference to a heavenly king who is throned in splendour is not a literal use of the words 'king' or 'throne', and however true it is that words such as 'shepherd', 'lord' and 'father' assert something genuine about the divine, we can appreciate that these are words with ordinary, 'earthly' meanings, used in an unusual, and perhaps metaphoric way. Is it different with the word 'God'? Perhaps it is not as different as we may suppose. We may have vague notions of giant supermen somewhere above the sky affecting things here on earth, and, after reducing them to one in our heads, speak of God as if we were using someone's ordinary name. But are we not doing with the vague notion of a god what we do with our notion of shepherds and kings—suggesting that the great mystery at the heart of things is in some respects like these (and like the other names we use in the same way)?

There is a great wisdom in the custom of earlier generations to speak of 'the One above', 'the Shepherd of our souls', or, with pious subtlety, to employ the word 'Heaven' as another synonym or signpost of the inexpressible, as in

Large was his bounty and his soul sincere,
Heaven did a recompense as largely send:
He gave to Misery all he had, a tear,
He gained from Heaven ('twas all he wished) a friend.

(Thomas Gray: 'Elegy')

In the Old Testament such use of metaphors, and the accompanying reluctance to speak directly of Jehovah, remind us that the attitude is not so much the expression of fastidious modern scepticism as a sign of reverence and spiritual sensitivity. Scepticism and mysticism are not necessarily enemies or even competitors. Religious claims with no hint that we fumble in a mystery too deep for the probing of precise analysis are more of a menace than a witness to faith.

'God' is a practical word, much more than a theoretical word. We use it, and the other words like 'Lord', 'Father', 'Shepherd' and 'King', as we bring ourselves and our circumstances into the dimension of all-embracing providence and grace. As these images and metaphors help us to set ourselves within a perspective that enables us to look at life in trust and hope, we become concerned less with speculating about the existence of an objective deity than with bringing ourselves into that gracious field of life where we are accepted, welcomed and affirmed. The distinction between objective and subjective is somehow transcended, when the disposition is one of worship rather than one of curiosity or detached enquiry. Just as there are words for use in love between people, so there are words for use in worship. You can, in both cases, use the words at other times; but you are then using them in a secondary, and not their primary, function. To say 'Almighty God' in a prayer is therefore rather like 'My darling', in the sense that they are both terms for use in appropriate situations.

To believe in God the Father Almighty is to trust God the Father Almighty—that is to say, in a Christian context, when we are re-orientated to a perspective of universal providence and hope, we are entitled to regard our relationship to that as a personal one ('Father'), the details and content of which are given to us in many ways, chiefly in Jesus Christ. If we proceed from regarding our relationship as personal to calling the 'other partner' in the relationship by personal terms ('Father'), we would be wise to think that God is at least personal, not that he is a person in exactly the same way we are people. Any further account of the mysterious reality or dimension to which we roughly apply the term 'God' must require attention to all the parts of the Creed without exception. It would be the height of absurdity to try to confine our thinking about any part of the Creed to that part. They are all bound up with each other. Most centrally the chief account of 'God' is Jesus.

If the Creed suggests to us a focus trust or background trust that is possible for us, and offers the life of Jesus as the more precise indication of the nature of that trust, we may think of 'the Father Almighty, Maker of Heaven and Earth' as a general summary of the nature and scope of the trust that is available to be exercised by us. It is a trust which will involve two elements, each profoundly important. One element is that it will be universally applicable, giving some unity and wholeness to all experience; and that is represented by the phrase 'Maker of heaven and earth'. Another element is that the trust will involve a relationship that is personal, like that of a child to a parent; and that is represented by the word 'Father'. (The important thing is that the relationship is personal, not that it is modelled on the child–father, rather than child–mother, husband–wife, or friend–friend relationship. Child–parent relationships vary greatly, and the word 'father' can have unhelpful as well as benign associations.)

One thing more might be said. For many of our predecessors heaven was highly populated, and hell also. Angels and saints and demons were all accepted as part of the mysterious world hidden from our physical world though deeply connected to it. The High King of Heaven in the hymn 'Be Thou my Vision' was, like the High King of Ireland, surrounded by lesser potentates and servants and messengers. I wonder if we are able to dispense with all the heavenly host and continue to employ the notion of the High King. Should we perhaps consider some of the modern ways in which mysterious powers of good and evil are represented and ask how the unifying focus—'God'—may be articulated in today's terms? The suggestion may sound dangerous. More dangerous to living faith, however, may be the assumption that we can drain heaven of its traditional environment and expect the central feature to stay credible.

4

Maker of Heaven and Earth

ONCE upon a time there were two people. One of them seemed very religious, and talked frequently with friends and strangers about God, the Bible, and the doctrines of the Christian faith. That person was particularly devoted to a 'literal' interpretation of the first chapter of the Book of Genesis, and argued that you could not be a Christian if you did not believe that the entire universe was made by God in six days. The same person was successful in business, with two fine houses and large investments, including some in overseas mining enterprises which were widely criticised both for exploiting workers on tiny wages and for leaving massive devastation of the environment with incalculable long-term consequences. The other person had little apparent interest in religion, found little meaning in any talk about God, and regarded the six day creation claim as manifest nonsense. This second person, unlike the first, gave most of his income away to people in need, spent days watching and learning the ways of animals and birds, and devoted hours to encouraging young people in respect and responsible stewardship of the natural environment. Which of these two, do you suppose, was closer to understanding a Christian approach to creation? If in practice you treat the world as if you had made it yourself, what purpose is served by your claiming that the same world was made by God (in however many days you like)?

The word 'Almighty' provides a good link between 'Father' which precedes it and 'Maker of heaven and earth' which follow it. It is an expression of praise, a shout of adoration, appropriate to that orientation of ourselves towards a perspective of deep and integrating trust which is the heart of believing and/or worshipping. As we require earthly pictures or models to speak of, or to, that which is beyond and through our sensory experience, it is only to be expected that human relationships (such as that of a child to a father) and the entire universe (in whole or part) should provide these pictures or models. Like seeing the sun through a stained glass window, the detail of our worship remains the details of our experience, but illuminated by something more, and revealing the 'something more' through the detail. To say 'Almighty' as we find these earthly things shot through with 'something more' or even 'something most', is to attribute to the 'something most' the quality of being fundamental, all-embracing, 'centre and soul of every sphere'. (The word 'Almighty' in the English translation of the Creed is in the Greek *pantocrator* and in Latin *omnipotens*. The Greek word is not found in many writers, and in the Greek version of the Old Testament it usually translates the Hebrew *Sabaoth* which means 'of hosts' in the phrase 'the Lord of Hosts'. The hosts were originally the armies of Israel, but came to mean the heavenly hosts of angels. The origin of the word 'Almighty' therefore supports the view that it was used not to mean 'God can do anything you care to imagine', but 'God is in the realm of the greatest and most splendid glory'.)

Even if 'God the Father Almighty, Maker of Heaven and Earth' is to be regarded as appropriate to worship and the exercise of trust, rather than in the context of detached enquiry or scientific investigation, we can still reasonably ask what the phrase 'Maker of Heaven and Earth' means in worship and believing. One thing we ought to do at the start is refuse to reduce the biblical background on the subject to the first chapter of Genesis which, if taken alone, can mislead us gravely about the Hebrew and the

Christian teaching in the Bible on this theme. In two respects that familiar account of God making the world in six days—which despite its place in the Bible is by no means the earliest part of the Old Testament—could leave us with a distorted view of the attitude to creation in Scripture. The first is that the Biblical writers on the whole seem much more interested in the divine power through the natural world and the world of human affairs than in saying how exactly the world was made or how long it took. The second is that they saw the presence of God not in the world's origin only but in its continuous preservation. They were not concerned with scientific accounts of how the world began. What mattered to them was the divine power through human affairs and the world of nature.

Two great connections need to be made, one between worship and wholeness, the other between creation and redemption. You will notice that the creed refers to the Maker not of earth only, but of heaven as well. Therefore the relationship of fundamental or 'focus' trust in worship is a relationship which somehow enables us to be connected to everything. Our lives, our minds, our feelings are known to be part of something great and universal, which does not swamp our littleness but rather gives us our deepest significance. The personal trusting or believing is related to the whole of reality, physical and spiritual, and worship is something which sets us in better perspective in relation to the whole world, physical and spiritual, individual and universal. That means in part that church on Sunday is a time for bringing all the things we have seen and heard about the world, near and far, good and dreadful, and letting ourselves be led into a disposition towards them which is in the direction of harmony with the signpost themes of the Creed.

The other connection is between creation and redemption. The Christian religion has made the work of redemption in Christ one of its chief themes, and that is not surprising. There is, however, a great danger in concentrating so devotedly on the wonderful medicine that you underestimate the value of the person who has been healed. If we speak of the redemption of the world in Christ, we are surely testifying to the value of a world which was good and suitable for redeeming. Whatever be the truth behind the term 'original sin', the beginning of the Book of Genesis allows and encourages us to speak of original goodness. Divine grace welcomes, affirms, and renews us, both in encouraging our goodness and in transforming or overcoming our badness. Focus on forgiveness of sin to the neglect of the consecration of goodness can lead to an atmosphere which is reminiscent of people refusing to leave hospital even after they are fit and well. A Christian approach to the 'making' of heaven and earth will encourage us to expect goodness in people and things (and in ourselves) and to seek restoration when the goodness is diseased.

It is for some of us too easy to talk romantically about the wonders of nature—the starry skies, the deep blue sea, the heather in bloom, the fertile meadows, the flowers and animals and birds. I happily share the wonder, and wish we spent more time in such situations of peace and beauty which kindle and restore our souls. But no amount of appreciation of the magnificence of the natural world should stand in the way of admitting that, to a huge extent, our attitude to the world is demonstrated not in occasional excursions to beauty spots, but in our continued financial and political priorities and practices.

5

And in Jesus

LOOKING back across thirty years (at least) of trying to read, listen, and think about the Christian religion, I have the impression that if people were asked thirty years ago what the irreducible heart of Christianity was, a fair proportion would say 'Jesus', whereas nowadays it seems that they would be more likely to say 'God'. Whether the observation is accurate, representative, or deeply significant, I do not know. It is certainly the case the people from time to time tell me that although they rarely go to church they 'believe in God' or 'believe that there is a God', but I cannot recall any in recent years referring to 'Jesus'. It is also the case that thirty years ago there were people speaking and writing about 'Jesus the Man' in a way which suggested that the notion of God might be outdated and redundant, but the significance of Jesus was powerful and contemporary. 'Religionless Christianity' and 'The Man for Others' were only two of the phrases which expressed that milieu. It seems that things have changed.

One ingredient in the making of the change could be that increasingly people may think of the Church as services of worship which they attend more or less occasionally, without attachment to congregations or involvement in Church 'membership'. Such an attitude may be accompanied by recognising that 'God' is *a*, or *the*, word which indicates worship, and which, in a Christian context, carries with it the appropriate references to the things of Christ. To a large extent I am encouraged by such an attitude, especially in preference to the notion of the Church as a list of members, with a clear distinction between those whose names are on the list and others. One of its dangers, however, is that worship may be seen as occasional bouts of vaguely religious sentiment, without the content and claim of that which is specifically Christian. It is not enough to 'assume' the things of Christ. They require to be allowed to confront us and inform us and renew us.

Another reason for the switch (if there is one) from 'Jesus' to 'God' may be the increased awareness of other religions in countries where previously the Christian Church was the only form of organised religious observance available in almost every place. To reckon that Muslims and Jews share with Christian people the worship of God is something that seems right and good (and I wish more Christian people knew that the word *Allah* is the Arabic word for 'God'). Little benefit in mutual understanding, however, is likely to result from Christian people playing down the specifically Christian elements in their religion, and thereby puzzling Islamic friends who expect any enjoyment of common factors to be accompanied by continuous learning of the details of one's own religious inheritance.

When we come to the words in the Creed, *and in Jesus Christ*, we could meditate and muse for endless years upon the significance of the word 'and'. The word often means much more than the fact that one thing is followed by another. (Think of the force of the word *et* in *Et tu, Brute,* or the contrived absurdity of 'The great Queen Anna, whom three realms obey, doth sometimes counsel take, *and* sometimes tea'.) Even when we say, 'I have great confidence in Dr Cameron, *and* in Dr Finlay', the extent to which our confidence is placed equally in both of them is liable to be conveyed by the tone of voice in which we pronounce the word 'and'. To say that we believe in 'God the Father Almighty, Maker of Heaven and Earth, and in Jesus Christ' is not to say that here are two people in whom we believe equally. It might be nearer the truth of the matter if we were to say 'I believe in God … who is Jesus Christ', or 'I believe in God … who is known through Jesus Christ'; but in neither alternative is it as straight-forward as that. Each of these alternative ways of putting it, how-ever, contributes a fair indication of Christian conviction. We must bear in mind that a Christian interpretation of 'God', 'Father Almighty' and 'Maker of Heaven and Earth' will rely on every word of the Creed, and is not confined to the opening phrases. It is not the case that we first get our understanding of God straight-ened out, and then proceed to think about Jesus. It is truer to say that Jesus is our description of God, than to say that we describe God and then go on to describe Jesus.

When we say that Jesus is our description of God we will mean by that—at least in part—that the first part of the Creed (before the name of Jesus) will provide an important framework for the way we speak about Jesus. Jesus will give content and spirit to practical believing, personal worship, universal rele-vance, and wholeness of being.

(1) *Practical Believing:* The sort of belief which matters—the sort that is meant when we say 'I believe in God'—is a trust-ing approach to life, a disposition of hope. The things which we learn about Jesus assist us in being welcomed into such a way of life, especially as in worship our minds, imaginations, and whole personalities are introduced and re-introduced to the spirit of Jesus Christ through the detail of his inheritance in the Church.

(2) *Personal Worship:* To have that trust and hope based on a personal relationship with the Holiest of all, we do not need to be able to think of a perfect person in the heavens and imagine what that person must be like. Christian worship consists more of adopting the attitudes appropriate to that Holy One, and regarding

the life and legacy of Jesus as the details to 'fill in' what might, if it were possible, be our picture of God.

(3) *Universal Relevance:* To speak of the focus of our trust as a Father who is Almighty, the Maker of Heaven and Earth, is to affirm the personal character of our relationship and the universal significance of that relationship. Jesus is not a road into a esoteric world of special religious reality, but the road towards a responsiveness to all life which helps us to appreciate its goodness and regard its need with love.

(4) *Wholeness of Being:* In worship, the reordering of our perspective applies not only to the universe as a whole, but to our individual lives. The two are interrelated. When the elements of our own personal composition are out of balance, our perspective on the world round about us reflects the imbalance. The things of Christ help us to move towards wholeness of being, not least by helping us to regard the wider world in all its brokenness as capable of being seen in some measure as a whole living unity.

The 'Author and Finisher of our faith' is not easily described or his impact simply explained. Let us at least keep firm and strong that little bridge-word 'and' before his name in the Creed.

6

Christ, His only Son, our Lord

WHEN we say the words 'and in Jesus Christ, his only Son, our Lord', we are using 'titles' for Jesus rich in association and import, and we are drawn into the Old Testament background to the Gospel. As we explore the way in which Jesus took and developed existing ideas, we begin to appreciate that the words themselves without their specific hinterland could leave us seriously ill-informed or misguided in our effort to grasp something of the dynamic subtlety of our Christian inheritance.

The world 'Christ' means 'anointed'. It is the Greek equivalent of the Hebrew *Messiah*. To be anointed—that is, to have oil put on your skin in a special ceremony—was the sign, among the Israelites as among other people, of appointment to a position of importance in the community, such as that of king or priest. The word came to refer to a high calling, a particular vocation, a divine designation for a purpose of significance. The belief grew in Old Testament times that there would appear a great leader and deliverer—the Messiah. The Christian Church said, and says, that Jesus was that Messiah.

When we ask what sort of 'anointed one' Jesus was, we are greatly helped by the second part of that long Old Testament book Isaiah—chapters 40-55, written in the sixth century BC, around a century and a half after the first 39 chapters. These later chapters contain descriptions of a 'servant' with whom Jesus appeared to identify himself. You might say that he modelled himself on the servant, or that he *was* the servant, or that the words about the servant were fulfilled in him—or all three. Two things about that servant stand out. The first is that he was humble, meek and endured great suffering. The second is that there seems to be a blurring of the distinction between one person and many people, between an individual and a corporate servant. Both are important for our understanding of Jesus' understanding of what it meant to be the special servant—the Christ.

To be the anointed one could seem to be a person of privilege, but Jesus came as one who serves. When you read the verses about the servant in Isaiah, you begin to wonder how far the character of Jesus bears remarkable similarity to the description of the servant, and how far your familiarity with the words from Isaiah have coloured your reading of the Gospels (which have vastly fewer personal details about Jesus than you would expect in a modern biography). 'He shall not cry, nor lift up, nor cause his voice to be heard in the street. A bruised reed shall he not break, and the smoking flax shall he not quench: he shall bring forth judgment unto truth' (Isaiah 42:2,3). Things deeper than the attribution of meekness are found in the hauntingly beautiful Isaiah 53, which speaks not only of the servant's meekness and of his suffering ('He is despised and rejected of men; a man of sorrows and acquainted with grief'), but also of his suffering and death becoming the instrument of our salvation and health (which are to some extent the same thing). 'Surely he hath borne our griefs and carried our sorrows.' 'He was wounded for our transgressions ... and with his stripes we are healed.' Very early on in Christianity Jesus was seen as redeemer and humble exemplar, echoing the union of these ideas in that part of Isaiah.

What I called the blurring of the distinction between an individual servant and a corporate servant or servant group seems deeply important for our understandng of the relationship between Christ and his disciples, or Christ and the Church, or even between

Christ and his Body (when 'Body' is not confined to the Church as commonly understood). He said, 'I am the light of the world' and also, 'You are the light of the world'. His special character is too readily defined in terms of uniqueness, whereas he seemed opposed to a 'Jesus the great hero' movement, and promoted the loving community as the instrument of his purpose and presence. This anointed one defines his style of messiahship, his Christhood, in terms of vicarious death and of departing as singular leader in order that the community might be inspired to be his 'body'.

The blurring of the distinction between Jesus and his disciples comes again when we think of 'His Only Son'. Chapter 3 of the First Epistle of St John begins:

Behold, what manner of love the Father hath bestowed upon us, that we should be called the sons of God: therefore the world knoweth us not, because it knew him not.

Beloved, now are we the sons of God, and it doth not yet appear what we shall be: but we know that, when he shall appear, we shall be like him; for we shall see him as he is.

The whole people of Israel had been described as the son of God ('When Israel was a child, then I loved him, and called my son out of Egypt'—Hosea 11:1). Both before and after Jesus, therefore, we find the notion of people as individuals and as a company being called the son or sons of God. In the Gospels the phrase 'Son of God' is used with the same sort of meaning as 'Christ', with the special additional element of personal devotion of Son to Father and personal 'family likeness' of Son to Father. Calling God 'Father' (or directing our worship to a Jesus-like one whom we can call Father) is doing what Jesus did, so that Jesus is both the example and the content of personal devotion to a Jesus-like Father. (Need it be said that Jesus was son of God in a way different from the way in which we are sons and daughters of our parents?) It might be added that 'only' and 'only-begotten' have the same sort of air as 'beloved'—as in 'This is my beloved Son'. Poetically they express devotion to Jesus' special place.)

When we speak of Jesus as 'our Lord', we run some fairly important risks. One is the danger of possessiveness in 'our', for the remaking of Christ as suits our place and time is a constant temptation, tantalisingly close to the imaginative duty of using the circumstances and insights of our place and time to help us notice things about Christ which we had previously ignored (which is different from remaking him to suit us). Another risk is that of what Neitzsche called the 'slave morality', a devotion to Christ which freezes our powers and makes impossible the fulfilment of his saying that 'I am come that ye might have life, and have it more abundantly'. A third risk is the removal from our devotion of the details the Gospels give us about Jesus, with the result that Jesus is nothing more or less than an alternative word for God, defined not by his life but by some vague notion of what a God should be like. Perhaps the best summary of a Christian understanding of Jesus as our Lord is in St John's Gospel, chapter 13:

Ye call me Master and Lord: and ye say well; for so I am. If I then, your Lord and Master, have washed your feet, ye also ought to wash one another's feet.

For I have given you an example, that ye should do as I have done to you. Verily, verily, I say unto you, The servant is not greater than his lord; neither he that is sent greater than he that sent him.

24

If ye know these things, happy are ye if ye do them.

To that I add only this: I readily accept these words as part of St John's interpretation of the situation, but I find the notion of Jesus speaking like that considerably at variance with the message conveyed.

7

Conceived by the Holy Ghost
Born of the Virgin Mary

PERSISTING in the notion that the Creed is practical, I possibly appear to compound persistence with perversity when I suggest that the words 'conceived by the Holy Ghost, born of the Virgin Mary' not only present no embarrassment to the notion, but splendidly confirm it. I have said that in some ways the saying of the Creed is like the singing of hymns, and this part of the Creed bears out such a comparison, both in the corporate, communal character of each activity, and also in the essential ingredient in hymns and Creeds of specific, concrete images which may, of course, be translated into more abstract doctrinal claims, but can never be reduced to them. Believing is too often regarded as the holding of opinions, not often enough as the inhabiting of an environment of nourishing imagery. (Mrs Kennedy Fraser is said to have been challenged after talk on fairies and sprites and elves and such like, 'Do you believe that these things are fact?' She replied, 'Do you not know that to the Celtic mind truth is more important than fact?')

Conception by the Holy Spirit and the birth by the Virgin Mary are two of the snow posts of imagery which Christian people have found to be helpful guides on the journey of faith which is Christian believing. To ask what they 'really' mean could seem like an invitation to ask what King Lear 'really' means, and could have the result of providing doctrinal-cum-moralistic summaries such as can pass for biblical preaching. Like other works of imaginative art, including the parables of Jesus, these pieces of imagery invite responses of open attentiveness accompanied by a deliberate reluctance to summarise them rapidly or reach definitions of their truth or consequences. Such things take time.

At the time when the Apostles' Creed was in the process of assembly, in the early centuries of Christianity, two ideas were going the rounds, each of which was regarded by the leaders of the Church as liable to lead people away from the road of Christian believing. Two snow posts were therefore required, one on each side of the road, since the two ideas suggested opposite lines of departure from the Christian path. The first cast doubts on the divinity of Jesus, and the second cast doubts on his humanity. 'Conceived by the Holy Ghost' and 'Born of the Virgin Mary' stand as signposts advising the pilgrim of the best path to take. Even as we proceed now to attempt to 'explain' how they serve that purpose, it is good for us to keep at the back of our minds the manner in which we receive their truth when we sing such lines as,

Christ, by highest heaven adored,
Christ, the everlasting Lord,
Late in time behold him come,
Offspring of a virgin's womb.

Or, in the translation of the Gaelic hymn written in Bunessan on the Isle of Mull, where I had my first home,

Child in the manger,
Infant of Mary,
Outcast and stranger,
Lord of all.

A distinguished theologian said that it was his regular practice on Christmas Day and on Easter Day to attend a church service in which no sermon was preached. While some of us might not go as far as that, we could all be assisted in the way we keep these days by the recognition that their huge profound mysteries are testified in song and poetry, colour and ceremony, to an extent which rational analysis or definition could never reach.

What 'Conceived by the Holy Ghost' was intended to convey was the conviction that Jesus did not *become* the Christ at some stage in his life—possibly after his resurrection—but that he was the Christ throughout his life from the very beginning. In practice that means that the whole life of Jesus provides for us the meeting point where heaven and earth come together, where we see and know the character of the One whom we worship, the point at which we receive a consecrating, liberating, and renewing grace. What 'Born of the Virgin Mary' was intended to convey was the conviction that the life of Jesus Christ was a fully human life, that he did not spend these thirty years as a sort of celestial space-man masquerading as an earth-man, but that the meeting point of God and people was a life which shared our human nature. (The word 'Virgin' is not nearly as important here as the words 'born of ... Mary'.) When we put these two phrases together, we find in them the thoroughly practical claim that the human life of Jesus—all of it—offers us the possibility of setting our human lives within the context of a providence of grace which bestows on us wholeness of being and freedom to trust and love.

Let me make three comments, about the Incarnation, the Virgin Birth, and the Holy Communion. When we think of the whole life of Christ as the point of our meeting with God, are we right to regard the Incarnation, the taking of human flesh by God, as a specific event identified either by Our Lord's conception or by his birth? Might it not be better to think of his whole human life as the Incarnation? Instead of it being a quasi-magical 'Hey Presto! God becomes man!' sort of thing, we could say, 'so far as I am concerned, the Incarnation means that I can look at the life of Jesus and regard that life as the expression of the divine, the heavenly Father, the heart and soul of the universe!' When we do that, our attitude to the focus of our worship cannot be detached from the attitudes of Jesus to people and life, whereas an identification of the Incarnation with Christmas can all too easily lead to a reverence for Jesus by name without any devotion to the things he said and did, or to the practical perspective he demonstrated.

What about the word 'Virgin'? Did Jesus have a human father? St Matthew and St Luke thought not; St John appeared to accept Joseph as his father; St Paul says he was born of a woman without mentioning the virginal claim; and St Mark says nothing about it at all. Some people find the idea helps them to believe in Christ, others find it hinders belief, and some take it or leave it. What is unfortunate, or even tragic, is when either the assertion or the denial of the human paternity leads to a neglect of the great claim of this part of the Creed—that Christ's whole life is the place of meeting of the human and the divine. And if there is a suggestion of deep mystery and great wonder, are we not right to regard him in such a way? Is it not one of his gifts that we are led to regard all people, and all life, as things of deep mystery and great wonder?

It is no accident that the chief and characteristic act of the Christian Church, the Holy Communion, brings us a mingling of our lives with the life of Christ. Just as the Incarnation can helpfully be seen as describing the entire life of Our Lord, so his words 'This is my Body' and 'This is my Blood' can be regarded as the equivalent of 'This is my life'. When we hear the words 'This is the body of Christ', it might be good for us to hear a fuller form, like 'Here is the whole life of Christ offered to you. In receiving this you are offered his whole experience to flow

29

into your experience and mingle with it'. There in the practice of worship we assert what lies behind 'Conceived by the Holy Ghost, born of the Virgin Mary'—the mingling of our experience with Christ's experience, and therefore with that which is central, which restores our balance and re-asserts our true position, which tilts us towards wholeness. Nothing could be more practical, more useful, more profoundly workable.

8

Suffered under Pontius Pilate
Was crucified, dead and buried

DOES it seem strange to you that the name of Pontius Pilate is included in the Creed? Only three human names are mentioned —Jesus, Mary and Pontius Pilate—in this short statement which appears to leave out so much of what seems important about Jesus: his teaching and healing, his disciples, the Last Supper, the transfiguration, his open friendship with reprobates, his calling of children. Yet day by day in Churches all round the world, Christian people say or sing the name of Pontius Pilate. Peter and Paul are not mentioned, nor Bethlehem, Galilee, Jerusalem. Why then should Pilate occupy such a position in the worship of the Church?

The question should not be regarded as more important than it is. Even if you look on the Creed as divinely inspired, it remains the product of human minds, and reflects the circumstances which produced it, with the inevitable rough edges and imperfections if judged by some imaginary standard of heavenly perfection. We are not obliged to find a good and sufficient reason for its selection of some things and its exclusion of others. It is therefore from a fairly relaxed position that we ask why Pontius Pilate is there.

Long before the Creed took the form in which we know it, the phrase 'suffered under Pontius Pilate' may have been quite common, and once a phrase enters common usage it is rarely subject to critical examination. People are given nicknames for many strange reasons and years later they are known in such words by people who could not begin to tell you what the nickname means. (Unlike the case of the Welsh police constable known as 'Jones Book and Pencil' who was promoted to sergeant and became known as 'Jones Book and Biro'.) The language of religion, like words in other contexts, comes to us more fuzzy than clear-cut, bearing the marks of the places and people and times by which it has come to us. Yet, why is Pilate in the Creed?

It is not because he made Jesus suffer pain. The phrase 'suffered under Pontius Pilate' did not mean 'endured agony on account of Pontius Pilate', but rather 'was condemned to death during the period when Pilate had authority'. The phrase is not included to extract sympathy from us for Jesus, or hatred for Pilate. The phrase is more like a date than a judgment. It records that the death of Jesus occurred during the period of years, around 30 AD, when Pontius Pilate was governor or procurator of Jerusalem and the surrounding country within the Roman Empire. The fact that the death of Jesus could be dated in terms of the administration of the Roman Empire may also have been in the minds of some of those who used it first. It gave the event a wider and more generally acceptable reference by which to fix it as a real event which truly happened.

Three times we say that Jesus died: when we say that he was crucified, when we say that he was dead, and when we say that he was buried—four times if the phrase 'suffered under Pontius Pilate' includes the sentence of death. For us today, it is unnecessary to say of anyone who lived in the past that he died. But there were people in ancient times whose very devotion to Jesus led them to doubt the humanity of his nature. Therefore the Church insisted that he was born of Mary and that he really and truly died. Not only did the Church wish to declare that Jesus was human, being born and dying as we all are born and die. They also wished to declare that his resurrection followed genuine death, and that he had not been translated in some mysterious way from the cross to his Easter form without death.

Of all the parts of the Creed this seems to be the only one which involved no element of faith, because suffering under Pilate, being crucified, dead and buried, are facts which require no religious perspective in order to accept them. But we must not forget the Creed's first words, 'I believe in', which sets everything that follows in the perspective of practical trust as well as the assertion of truth. When we say that we believe in Jesus who suffered under Pontius Pilate, was crucified, dead, and buried, we are saying that we seek to live in an attitude of trust and hope and security of spirit which are encouraged in by us what we know about Jesus, his living and his dying.

It appears that the death of Christ on the cross has been so powerful a theme of meditation and devotion among Christian people that it might be suggested that what happened before and what happened after Good Friday are virtually peripheral to that central focus. It is certainly the case that the greater part of the four Gospels of Matthew, Mark, Luke and John is devoted to the last days of Our Lord's life, so much so that they have been described as Passion Narratives with introductions. It would, however, be quite wrong to say that the character and teaching of Jesus are treated as if they scarcely mattered (despite the emphasis of St Paul). The man who died was the man who lived, and the impact of his death was the impact of his life. Equally it would be wrong to suggest that meditating upon the death of Christ diminished the significance of his Easter presence; for Christian people have held not only that they were benefited by their dwelling on Christ's cross, but that the benefit was ministered to them by a divine power greater than themselves. 'From the cross the radiance streaming adds more lustre to the day.'

To some extent the story of Christianity has been the story of the impact of the cross. The interpretations of its significance have come and gone, expressing their place and time, and the cross has risen above them. More than any other interpretation is the one which Jesus himself gave, when he took bread and a cup of wine, in the context of the passover thanksgiving for liberation, and led his disciples to hold, as millions since have held, that 'every time you eat this bread and take this cup, you do shew forth the Lord's death until he come'.

9

He descended into Hell;
the third day
He rose again from the dead

ONE of the first statements about the resurrection of Jesus Christ
to be found in the New Testament, earlier than the four Gospels of
Matthew, Mark, Luke and John, occurs in the first Epistle of St
Paul to the Corinthians, at chapter 15:

*Moreover, brethren, I declare unto you the gospel which I
preached unto you, which also ye have received, and wherein
ye stand;*

*By which also ye are saved, if ye keep in memory what I
preached unto you, unless ye have believed in vain.*

*For I delivered unto you first of all that which I also received,
how that Christ died for our sins according to the scriptures;*

*And that he was buried, and that he rose again the third day
according to the scriptures:*

And that he was seen of Cephas, then of the twelve:

*After that, he was seen of about five hundred brethren at
once ....*

After that, he was seen of James; then of all the apostles.

And last of all he was seen of me also, as of one born out of due time.

For I am the least of the apostles, that am not meet to be called an apostle, because I persecuted the Church of God.

But by the grace of God I am what I am.

St Paul goes on to say how important for Christian faith belief in the resurrection is:

If Christ be not raised, your faith is vain; ye are yet in your sins.

And then St Paul in a poetic outburst of conviction affirms the vast scope and implication of the resurrection as he understands it:

If in this life only we have hope in Christ, we are of all men most miserable.

But now is Christ risen from the dead, and become the firstfruits of them that slept.

For since by man came death, by man came also the resurrection of the dead.

For as in Adam all die, even so in Christ shall all be made alive.

What are we to think of these things? Are we expected to believe in the resurrection, and, if we are, what does the phrase 'believe in the resurrection' mean? What does the word 'resurrection' mean? I think that it is greatly to the credit of the writers of the New Testament that none of them attempts to describe the resurrection of Jesus. Nobody says that at a quarter to three in the morning his heart started beating, or that sometime between four and five o'clock his old dead body was transformed into a different sort of body. They just say that he rose, or that he was raised, or that God raised him. You will not miss the fact that rising is here a figurative or metaphorical term, and no one speaks of moving upwards in a literal sense any more than the phrase 'descended into hell' was used to refer to a literal descent anywhere, since it means no more than that he was really and truly dead. It is perfectly accurate to say that the first event which Paul claims in unfigurative terms is the event of Christ being seen by disciples, though there too no attempt is made to say how that occurred. They were sure that they had seen the old Jesus, and seen him in a new way. Is that not astonishing enough?

It is easier to suggest some of the things resurrection does *not* mean, than to be precise about what it *does* mean. It does not mean immortality of the soul and it does not mean resuscitation of the body. Immortality of the soul was not a notion acceptable to the Hebrew mind, and the Church was most emphatic in its claim that Jesus had genuinely died; no part of him remained alive. So far as resuscitation of the body is concerned, no claim is made that that is what happened; and the witness of the apostles that the Jesus whom they saw after Easter could appear and vanish through closed doors, together with the inability of the disciples on the road to Emmaus to recognise him, must rule out any definition of resurrection as resuscitation, a coming back to life in his former way. If we consider the question of whether we believe that the resurrections 'happened', what we should consider is whether we accept that the disciples saw Jesus after he had died (leaving out how it was possible).

It seems certain that whatever happened to the disciples gave them the confidence to stand for Christ and by him, and to regard his mission and ministry not as a failure, but as a triumph fit to be the basis of their lives and the hope of the world ready to be shared with everyone. Perhaps for some of us the situation is reversed, in that the teaching and spirit of Jesus before his crucifixion may be compelling and magnetic, but we find the resurrection hard to take. Instead of the resurrection confirming the authority and validity of Jesus to us, as it did for the disciples, it puzzles and disturbs us. It is therefore all the more important to say that we are invited not to believe in the resurrection, but to believe in Jesus Christ crucified and risen.

When we ask what it means to believe in Christ crucified and risen, we might find help in the account of the journey to Emmaus on the evening of Easter Day which we find in St Luke's Gospel, chapter 24. It is not only a beautiful piece of scripture, but can be seen as a parable about the Church's relationship with Christ; and it may have been written with that in mind. The mystery of resurrection is testified in their not knowing who he was. They came to know him through his opening to them the scriptures and his breaking of the bread—word and sacrament, as it has been ever since. We study the testimony of the first disciples, and hear again words from the four Gospels where his doings and sayings are given to us; and in the Holy Communion we put ourselves in the position of letting signs of his death become for us instruments of life and hope—hope that tells us the standards and perspective and spirit of Jesus are valid now and worthy of practice in private and public life, personal behaviour and political and professional priority. It is true that some of us will accompany these things with feelings which we might describe as knowledge of the risen Christ, whereas others will not. That should not cause us worry. What matters more is that adjustment in the direction of basic trust and wholesome living which is the heart of worship. These things may be better sung and practised than spoken.

Blessed be the God and Father of our Lord Jesus Christ, which according to his abundant mercy hath begotten us again unto a lively hope by the resurrection of Jesus Christ from the dead, to an inheritance incorruptible and undefiled, and that fadeth not away.

(1 Peter 1:3 and 4)

10

He ascended into Heaven, and sitteth on the right hand of God the Father Almighty

IF you are looking for nourishment of the soul, or seeking a larger, deeper awareness of the heart and scope of Christianity, you could do much worse than turn again to six hymns of Cecil Francis Alexander who lived from 1818 until 1895. Throw accusations at them if you like, of being Victorian, simplistic, schoolmarmish and moralistic. Even if the mud sticks, they all survive it and shine with a great deal to give us. She rewrote St Patrick's hymn in English, 'I bind unto myself today the strong name of the Trinity', with its huge sweep of life focussed on Christ at the heart of creation. She was also the author of three hymns which are among the best known and best loved upon three great Christian themes—'All things bright and beautiful' on God the Creator; 'Once in royal David's city' on the birth of Christ; and 'There is a green hill far away' on his death. She also wrote on the Holy Spirit—'Spirit of God that moved of old upon the water's darkened face'. And on the ascension, this particular hymn, 'The golden gates are lifted up', so expresses something important in our faith that I give it here in full:

The golden gates are lifted up,
The doors are opened wide;
The King of Glory is gone in
Unto His Father's side.

Thou are gone up before us, Lord,
To make for us a place,
That we may be where now Thou art,
And look upon God's face.

And ever on our earthly path
A gleam of glory lies;
A light still breaks behind the cloud
That veiled Thee from our eyes.

Lift up our hearts, lift up our minds;
Let Thy dear grace be given,
That, while we wander here below,
Our treasure be in heaven;

That where Thou art, at God's right hand,
Our hope, our love may be.
Dwell Thou in us, that we may dwell
For evermore in Thee.

What seems most right about that hymn—and there are others of which the same thing may be said—is that worship and practice are what matter, not purity of doctrine or intellectual persuasiveness. (You may of course hold that a doctrine is purest when it best serves worship and practice, and even that this is the way in which it is most persuasive.) What the Church says on the theme of the ascended Christ, it says better in bursts of praise than in detailed claims about precise events. In two passages in the Epistle to the Ephesians you find that note of praise combined, as in the hymn, with definite connection to practice, our daily lives and attitudes. In the first chapter we read:

Wherefore I also ... cease not to give thanks for you, making mention of you in my prayers; that the God of our Lord Jesus Christ, the Father of glory, may give unto you the spirit of wisdom and revelation in the knowledge of him: the eyes of our understanding being enlightened; that ye may know what is the hope of his calling, and what the riches of the glory of his inheritance in the saints, and what is the exceeding greatness of his power to us-ward who believe, according to the working of his mighty power, which he wrought in Christ when he raised him from the dead, and set him at his own right hand in the heavenly places, far above all principality and power and might and dominion and every name that is named, not only in this world but also in that which is to come: and hath put all things under his feet, and gave him to be the head over all things to the Church, which is his body, the fulness of him that filleth all in all.

The same celebration of comprehensive relevance is echoed in the fourth chapter of Ephesians:

There is one body and one spirit, even as ye are called in one hope of your calling; one Lord, one faith, one baptism, one God and Father of all, who is above all, and through all, and in you all. But unto every one of us is given grace according to the measure of the gift of Christ. Wherefore he saith, When he ascended up on high he led captivity captive, and gave gifts unto men. (Now that he ascended, what is it but that he also descended first into the lower parts of the earth? He that descended is the same also that ascended up far above all heavens, that he might fill all things.)

Apart from St Luke, the writers of the New Testament do not

42

speak of Christ's ascending forty days after Easter, or of the Church being inspired ten days after that, at Pentecost. The Christian calendar reflects St Luke, and doubtless much benefit follows. Yet I think some harm may come as well, for not only incredulity but thinness of believing may come from an exclusive concentration on the '40–50 sequence'. It would be good for us all—and deeply important for some of us—to set aside for a time the sequence that the resurrection 'happened' three days after the crucifixion, the ascension forty days after that, and the descent of the Spirit ten days thereafter, and try to catch some sense of the perspective on the life and death of Jesus which bathes his whole existence in glory and does not merely add the glory as an appendix to his life. Much mental effort has been devoted to defining and expressing the distinction between God and Jesus. In Christian worship and practice it is more important to see them as one, and saying that Jesus is at the right hand of God (God's right hand man) amounts to saying that for practical purposes you can regard Jesus as God—the whole life of Jesus, his teaching and attitude and spirit, as the focus of worship, of our sense of wholeness and our basic trust.

Martin Luther spoke of our having a brother in heaven. To say that 'he is at the father's side, the man of love, the crucified' is to assert the value of his humanity and therefore of all humanity. To speak of him as our priest is to regard his earthly life as the medium by which we are in contact with things fundamental and everlasting.

The language used about Christ in glory is heady stuff, involving imagery which will strike twentieth century minds as strange, unless they are accustomed to it. There is no benefit in being accustomed to it if it has lost its power for us. Yet reducing mystery by translating images, or by turning poetry into prose, may not be the way to proceed. Rather with awareness that we are dealing with mystery deep and essential can we sing and seek to live by such lines as:

Where high the heavenly temple stands,
The house of God not made with hands,
A great High Priest our nature wears,
The guardian of mankind appears.

Though now ascended up on high,
He bends on earth a brother's eye;
Partaker of the human name,
He knows the frailty of our frame.

With boldness, therefore, at the throne
Let us make all our sorrows known;
And ask the aids of heavenly power
To help us in the evil hour.

And, in the good and happy hour, to give us thankful hearts; and hopeful spirits at all times.

11

From thence
He shall come to judge
the quick and the dead

'FROM thence he shall come to judge the quick and the dead.'
'From thence' means 'from heaven', and 'quick' means 'living'.
We may therefore express this line in the Creed as 'from heaven
he shall come to judge the living and the dead'. Place and time
seem both to be involved, though in unusual ways. We know that
the notion of heaven as a place is different from the notion of
London as a place; and similarly the notion of a journey in time—
'he shall come'—is different from our regular understanding of
a journey in time, in, for example, 'I intend to go to London
tomorrow, and I shall come back to Edinburgh on Wednesday'. If
you accept that heaven is a place only in an odd understanding of
place, you may also accept that 'he shall come' refers to a journey
at some time or other only in odd senses both of making a journey
and of some time or other.

We must not forget that the line in the Creed which refers to
Christ's coming from heaven to judge the living and the dead—
that is, to judge everyone—is a line in the Creed, and therefore part
of an expression of trust more than of balanced opinion. What
we are not saying is, 'I think he will come from heaven to judge
the living and the dead', or 'It is my considered opinion that he will
come to judge the living and the dead'. We are saying, 'I believe
in God and in Jesus who will come to judge the living and the
dead'; or, more accurately, we are expressing a basic trust, a deep
hope, and holding as signs of the nature of that trust certain things

about Jesus. Included in these aspects of Jesus are his coming again and his judging. The question which we might usefully ask is, how do the themes of Christ's coming again, and of Christ's judgment, inform, enlarge, encourage that deep trust and lively hope which are the heart of belief in God and therefore of worship?

Perhaps the most helpful way to proceed is to travel in our minds to the season of Advent, the four weeks before Christmas, and recall the themes of that season, especially as they are expressed in the hymns we sing at that time. 'Advent' means 'coming', and that month before Christmas has been used for centuries by the Church as a time of double preparation—for the celebration of Our Lord's coming among us, in his birth at Bethlehem, and for his coming in power at the fulfilment, the consummation, the end. The fact that the two aspects of preparation merge in our advent hymns is important.

Lo! he comes, with clouds descending,
Once for favoured sinners slain,
Thousand thousand saints attending
Swell the triumph of his train;
Alleluia! Alleluia! Alleluia!
God appears on earth to reign.

We also sing:

Earth can now but tell the story
Of thy bitter cross and pain;
She shall yet behold thy glory,
When thou comest back to reign:
Christ is coming! Christ is coming!
Let each heart repeat the strain.

46

Imagery from the New Testament abounds in the great hymn 'Wake, awake, for night is flying', where we sing of the great wedding feast which is a theme of Jesus' parables about his kingdom:

Come forth ye virgins, night is past!
The bridegroom comes; awake,
Your lamps with gladness take;
Alleluia!
And for his marriage feast prepare,
For ye must go to meet him there.

and recall some words of St Paul when we sing:

Nor eye hath seen, nor ear
Hath yet attained to hear
What there is ours;
But we rejoice, and sing to thee
Our hymn of joy eternally.

If all the rich variety of picture and memory which the Advent hymns produce is to be summarised in one word, my choice would be the word 'fulfilment'. It would also be the word that I suggest as a summary of the themes of judgment and the coming again of the Lord. In the writing of the New Testament, and in hymns and meditation of the Church in subsequent centuries, people were groping after some way of holding together ideas which seem to be contradictory—the idea of fulfilment in our experience of wholeness here and now, the idea of something good for each of us when we die, and the idea of something comprehensively ful-filling for all people and all things at the end of time or beyond time. Also they tried to bring together goodness and grace, the importance of doing good with the fundamental awareness that all things are given to us and our goodness is not our achievement, for we rely not on our doing the right thing to bring us peace, but on mercy and generosity undeserved. When the notion of Christ the judge is held before us, we must understand there the idea of one who brings things to a state of rightness, rather than one who doles out praise and blame, prizes and punishment. We are called both to work for right and also to believe that the right is gift and not achievement. We are offered encouragement towards a sense of destiny, of all things working together for good; and if we use a story of creation at the start as a symbol of that, without holding the story to be factually accurate, why should we not employ some other stories which appear to be about the end of things, without regarding them as any more a matter of fact?

In the centre of such a sense of wholeness and justice is Jesus and his character. Beside the parable of the sheep and the goats, with its emphasis on surprise in both camps (and are we not all in both camps?), we must set the father of the prodigal son and see his welcome to his wayward son as the spirit of grace by which things come to their fulfilment.

Nowhere have I seen these mysteries more wonderfully set down in recent times than in the poem 'Transfiguration' by Edwin Muir, about the transfiguration of Christ. Here are the opening and closing sections:

So from the ground we felt that virtue branch
Through all our veins till we were whole, our wrists
As fresh and pure as water from a well,
Our hands made new to handle holy things,
The source of all our seeing rinsed and cleansed
Till earth and light and water entering there
Gave back to us the clear unfallen world.

......

Was it a vision?
Or did we see that day the unseeable
One glory of the everlasting world
perpetually at work, though never seen
Since Eden locked the gate that's everywhere
And nowhere?

......

But he will come again, it's said, though not
Unwanted and unsummoned; for all things,
Beasts of the field, and woods, and rocks, and seas,
And all mankind from end to end of the earth
Will call him with one voice. In our own time,
Some say, or at a time when time is ripe.
Then he will come, Christ the uncrucified,
Christ the discrucified, his death undone,
His agony unmade, his cross dismantled—
Glad to be so—and the tormented wood
Will cure its hurt and grow into a tree
In a green springtime corner of your Eden,
And Judas damned take his long journey backward
From darkness into light and be a child
Beside his mother's knee, and the betrayal
Be quite undone and never more be done.

12

I believe in the Holy Ghost

SOME years ago, on holiday in Anglesey, I noticed that the Welsh for 'Holy Spirit' was *Ysbryd Glan*. (The service was partly in English and partly in Welsh, and the Prayer Books were written in both languages.) I knew that in Scottish Gaelic the word *glan* meant 'clean', and although Welsh is not nearly as close to Scottish Gaelic as Irish Gaelic is, they are all Celtic languages. I wondered if the word for holy in Welsh could be the same as the word for 'clean' in Gaelic. It was an intriguing idea. Not many months later I had the good fortune to meet a biblical scholar of great repute who was a Welsh-speaking Welshman, and asked him about it. I was quite surprised to learn from him that the sense of the word in Welsh was close to its sense in Gaelic, and he quoted the phrase '*afon glan*' and told me that it meant a clear running river. Now I do not know what connections or associations the word 'holy' produces in your minds or in your imaginations, but ever since I heard about '*afon glan*' I have envied the Welsh if whenever they hear about Holy Spirit they are able to make some connection with a clear running river.

When the Spirit of God is spoken of in the Bible, ideas are often present not far removed from the sort of ideas suggested by a clear running river—liveliness, power, light, movement, and most certainly the quality of not being fixed or trapped or confined. The basic and oldest idea is not that of water, but rather of air—breath, wind—with the same association of life and power, movement and resistance to confinement. The first sentences in the Bible are:

50

In the beginning God created the heaven and the earth. And the earth was without form, and void; and darkness was upon the face of the deep. And the Spirit of God moved upon the face of the waters.

And God said, let there be light: and there was light.

In the third chapter of St John's Gospel, Jesus is quoted as saying:

The wind bloweth where it listeth, and thou hearest the sound thereof, but canst not tell whence it cometh, and whither it goeth: so is every one that is born of the Spirit.

These words from St John offer more than a repetition of the comparison of the Spirit to wind, air or breath. It is not just a comparison, a convenient, even illuminating, metaphor. In some way, Spirit is wind, air, and the breath we breathe, which indicates so wonderfully and terribly the difference between life and death. How can we understand it? Perhaps one clue is that the best route to an understanding of any thing, any person, any event, any element of experience, is the adoption of a responding attitude appropriate to whatever it is that we seek to understand. You don't 'understand' people in the same way as you 'understand' mathematical formulae. You don't 'understand' the Holy Spirit by defining, analysing, 'solving' its 'puzzle'. Words may come later. Permitting the mystery to affect you deeply must always come first and not go away. Our biggest obstacle in the matter of 'the Holy Spirit' is not our difficulty in making logical sense of the phrase, but our reticence in being open to the essential living wonder of things.

Even if some success may be achieved in articulating the

doctrine of the Trinity—God as Father, Son, and Holy Spirit—the temptation to read that doctrine into the biblical references to the spirit can have the effect of distorting powerful images, points, statements which need not suffer because of their being mutually irreconcilable. In St John's Gospel we find the Spirit associated with mystery, liberty, and surprise, in the growth of the disciples to be in some way more Christ-like and closer to Christ because his physical presence will be replaced by the Spirit in and among them in power and freedom and love. (I feel rather suspicious of the assumption that Christianity is more convincing to 'unbelievers' the more it is presented as 'simple'. Acceptance of a mystery beyond rational analysis carries a credibility which is not present when something is too clear to be true. Whatever else the doctrine of the Trinity may do for us, it should at least remind us that the Christian Church has long been aware that talk about God is not a straightforward or 'simple' thing.)

It is always a mistake to confuse mystery with mystification or with puzzle. When we see spring flowers growing and bursting into bloom, we can be full of a sense of wonder at the mystery of life without feeling obliged to seek a solution to some such puzzle as 'What is life?' Nor need we feel a greater sense of wonder at some freak event in nature than at the ordinary predictable marvels. There is often an inclination to identify the Holy Spirit with events that are strange, spectacular, unpredictable, and there is nothing wrong with that, so long as we are willing to identify the Spirit as fully, or more fully, with all life and all love and all grace. The apostles could speak of their inspiration at Pentecost as enabling them to engage in the strange gift of speaking with tongues, but also as leading them to the practice of community fellowship and sharing. St Paul's list of the fruits of the Spirit (in chapter 5 of the Epistle to the Galatians) has nothing esoteric or stupendous about it:

The fruit of the Spirit is love, joy, peace, longsuffering, gentleness, goodness, faith, meekness, temperance.

In the First Epistle to the Corinthians he speaks of the gifts of healing, teaching, preaching, and tongues, but goes on to urge his hearers to seek above all else the way of love:

Though I speak with the tongues of men and of angels, and have not charity, I am become as sounding brass, or a tinkling cymbal.

There are always religious people who appreciate the unusual more than the regular. It is good for the Church when the majority are not of that sort.

Perhaps I should express that differently. While emphasising the wonder and beauty of ordinary things and unspectacular graces, I do not for a moment suggest that our reaction to such things should be predictable or always the same, but rather that we should be willing to be surprised by fresh thankfulness for ordinary things, and new appreciation of the beauty of life. Particularly we should be willing to see new truth and find fresh vision in the things about Christ which we have known for years; such is the work of the Spirit.

To meditate upon the references to the Spirit in the Bible would take us hours—or rather would take a lifetime. Only one more thing I wish to say now: that in all its thinking about God as Father, Son and Holy Spirit, the Church has always been concerned to speak of the oneness of God, and therefore we need not feel guilty if we cannot think of the Holy Spirit as something like a separate person (in the normal sense of the word person). Of course the hymns and prayers and writings often speak as if that were so; but then they also speak of the Spirit as a mighty rushing wind or as a brooding gentle dove.

To say we believe in the Holy Ghost is to affirm that element in our basic trust which affirms the area of life and creativity, surprise and hope, fresh grace and new love, which come to us in many ways, find their focus in Christ Jesus, and are recognised as fundamental to the nature of the goodness of life and not chance aberrations from it.

13

The Holy Catholic Church

DO we believe in the Church? I mean, do we regard the Church as one of the great signposts on the journey of life, a vehicle of hope, a channel of wholeness and well-being for us? Many answers may be given to such a question, and they will occupy positions in a range from the highly positive to the highly negative. The highly positive reply might take the form of saying that asking Christian people if they believed in the Church is like asking a shoal of herring if they believe in the sea. It is their home, and essential to them. In it they find their food and travel on their journeys. Dangers lurk in it and weak nourishment as well as strong. But if Christian believing is a journey of hope and trust, the Church is an essential environment of nurture and belonging as surely as the great salt sea is the environment of the herring. That might be one positive answer.

In contrast I can readily hear a representative of the opposite view say, 'Not only does my Christian faith not need the Church, but I feel quite sure that my Christian faith would be harmed— or was harmed, or is harmed—by the Church. Faith for me is a personal and individual matter, and all the fuss and confusion and expense of Churches make it not easier but immeasurably more difficult'. That might be one negative answer to the question, Do you believe in the Church?

It is possible to combine the two replies and say that the Church is, or could be, a useful—even essential—facility for the transmission and encouraging of Christian believing, but that Christian believing is, by its nature, personal and individual. Yet, though the social and individual aspects of believing are surely important, I question whether they can be so easily distinguished, in the suggestion that the essence of faith is individual while its transmission and encouragement are social. It seems to me that there are social and individual elements in both—just as most important things about our spiritual, emotional, mental attitudes involve other people as well as ourselves. At the heart of Christian religion is the Holy Communion where what *we do* is more important that what *I think or feel*.

The American writer Frederick Buechner in his thoroughly refreshing book *Wishful Thinking*, the subtitle of which is 'A Theological ABC', writes the following entry under the word 'CHURCH':

The visible Church is all the people who get together from time to time in God's name. Anybody can find out who they are by going to look.

The invisible Church is all the people God uses for his hands and feet in this world. Nobody can find out who they are except God.

Think of them as two circles. The optimist says they are concentric. The cynic says they don't even touch. The realist says they occasionally overlap.

In a fit of high inspiration, the author of the Book of Revelation states that there is no temple in the New Jerusalem, thus squelching once and for all the tedious quip that since Heaven is an endless church service, anybody with two wits to rub together would prefer Hell.

The reason for there being no temple in the New Jerusalem is presumably the same as the reason for Noah's leaving the ark behind when he finally makes it to Mount Ararat.

Four things in Buechner's 'definition' invite further mention:

First, he speaks of the difficulty of defining the Church. That is important. Numbers are significant, but not the only significant factors in the strength or weakness of the Church. Activity in organising the Church may be important; but so is the presence of the Church inside your soul at your daily work. We should be suspicious of glib definitions of Church membership, its strength or weakness, especially of criteria which assess the Church as a recreational club or philanthropic association. The Church is people; but it is also the Bible and the sacraments, even buildings and paintings and poetry and music; and above all the Church is Christ. Definition is not merely difficult. It is impossible.

Second, the Church has its roots in the Old Testament, in Israel. There the distinction was not clear between the individual and the corporate personality of the community. There is little basis there for the idea that faith is private, individual, or in that sense personal.

Third, the notion of God's hands and feet takes us to the view of the Church as Christ's body, of which he is the head and we are members—members not in the sense of individuals choosing to join his group, but members as the parts of the body are members, without the possibility of separate existence as individuals. For St Paul, Christian faith was as social, communal, corporate as that. It is however our relationship to Christ that binds us together, in Paul's view, and not our relationship to each other that makes us Christian.

Fourth, the Church exists for its own redundancy. Jesus' kingdom offers a vision of all things brought to their fulfilment, people at one inside themselves, at one with each other, at one with all creation. Church is Church insofar as it renders us more human, more whole, and serves to indicate the good and right order of things to which our destiny calls us.

Worship is the heart of the Church, but the Church is more than services. Fellowship is important in the Church, but so is our relationship with all the community and world. To call the Church catholic is to testify to its comprehensiveness and universality, its breadth and scope. To call it holy is to affirm its relationship to Christ and its priestly function in relation to the wider world. Its past and its future are present in it, and the communion of saints is that sharing across the generations and the boundary of death in ways that are as mysterious as they are true. Some elements of that large understanding of Church—larger than a group of individuals or their opinions and efforts—is communicated in Edwin Muir's poem 'The Church', where he reflects on a new church building in America:

This autumn day the new cross is set up
On the unfinished church, above the trees,
Bright as a new penny, tipping the tip
Of the elongated spire in the sunny breeze,
And is at ease;
Newcomer suddenly, calmly looking down
On this American university town.

Someone inside me sketches a cross—askew,
A child's—on seeing that stick crossed with a stick,
Some simple ancestor, perhaps, that knew,
Centuries ago when all were Catholic,
That this archaic trick
Brings to the heart and the fingers what was done
One spring day in Judaea to Three in One;

When God and man in more than love's embrace,
Far from their heaven and tumult died,
And the holy Dove fluttered above that place
Seeking its desolate nest in the broken side,
And Nature cried
To see heaven doff its glory to atone
For man, lest he should die in time, alone.

I think of the Church, that stretched magnificence
Housing the crib, the desert, and the tree,
And the good Lord who lived on poverty's pence
Among the fishermen of Galilee,
Courting mortality,
And schooled himself to learn his human part:
A poor man skilled in dialectic art.

What reason for that splendour of blue and gold
For One so great and poor He was past all need?
What but impetuous love that could not hold
Its storm of spending and must scatter its seed
In blue and gold and deed,
And write its busy Books on Books of Days
To attempt and never touch the sum of praise.

I look at the church again, and yet again,
And think of those who house together in Hell,
Cooped by ingenious theological men
Expert to track the sour and musty smell
Of sins they know too well;
Until grown proud, they crib in rusty bars
The Love that moves the sun and the other stars.

Yet fortune to the new church, and may its door
Never be shut, or yawn in empty state
To daunt the poor in spirit, the always poor.
Catholic, Orthodox, Protestant, may it wait
Here for its true estate.
All's still to do; roof, window and wall are bare.
I look, and do not doubt that He is there.

A Church whose vision has less scope than that is not worthy of the attention of healthy and hopeful people; nor is it likely to help us where at heart we are unhealthy and hopeless.

14

The Communion of Saints

CHURCHES often bear the names of saints, and people some-times bear the names of qualities, attributes, dispositions—Joy, Ernest, Felicity, Amanda, Victor among them. We get accustomed to people having these names, and rarely ask ourselves how closely their personalities reflect their names. (How joyful is Joy, how happy Felicity?) We also get accustomed to St Bartholomew's, St James', St Mary's, St Bride's, and rarely ask ourselves how appropriate in each case is the assignation of saint to church. They are simply the names of churches. But it was not always so.

When the parish church of Edinburgh was dedicated to St Giles' (we do not know when first his name was so linked, though probably it was long before the dedication of 1243, when Bishop de Bernham included the place in his great list of churches being re-dedicated, or dedicated 'properly') the people of the town must surely have expected some practical benefits to come from the saint's patronage of their church. Dedication by a saint's name was an invocation of the saint's present protection, and no mere selection of a good-sounding name. But when the 'New Town' extension of Edinburgh was built at the end of the eighteenth century, and they called the two new town churches St Andrew's and St George's, they were doing something worlds away from the practical patronage of saints in heaven. They were marking the union of Scotland and England.

In Scotland, as in other countries strongly affected by the

Reformation, the cult of saints declined, although local fondness for local saints was not eradicated by central principles. The difference between the world of the twelfth century (approximately) and the changed environment of Enlightenment Europe should not be exaggerated, especially if there continued in the assumptions of people three features we can associate with devotion to saints.

The first is the acceptance of a well-populated heaven, where angels and saints inhabit the divine presence. The second is the recognition that people are inseparable from their ancestry, not least in faith and the knowledge of God. (To say of God that he is the God of Abraham, Isaac and Jacob is to say much more than that he is something which these three happened to have in common.) The third is the assumption that in some way those who have died are able to help us now—and that assumption surely continued in post-Reformation Scotland, not only in what might be called the Celtic fringe.

Is it not possible that with these three features the two worlds of mediaeval and eighteenth century 'Protestant' Europe may have shared the essence of devotion to the saints, despite the appearance to the contrary? Might they not have more in common with each other in that respect than either has in common with a world which lacks such a sense of a living mutual involvement of the past with the present? If the twentieth century has seen the growth of an ecumenical movement reminding Christian people of their membership of one universal Church, I wonder if the time has not come for the ecumenism of space to be joined by an ecumenism of time, in a recovery of the vital necessity of the living past as part of a more balanced and more catholic present. We may be glad that we are not trapped by the class or feudal status of our birth; but if we go to the opposite extreme and believe ourselves to be separate and distinct from the generations who preceded us, we may find ourselves in another trap—of an exaggerated and insular self-sufficiency which is neither sufficient for our need, nor likely to lead to freedom of the self.

Believing in the Communion of Saints amounts to much the same as believing in the Church, especially when three aspects of believing in the Church are brought into prominence. The first aspect is the connection of our relationship with Jesus Christ to our relationship with fellow believers. The Communion of Saints has been defined in several ways, and high on the list of definitions is the relationship which the inhabitants of heaven have with God, the Christ-like God. We who live in 'this world' are invited to participate in that communion of the saints with Christ. In a sense the primary communion is that which the saints—and we with them—have with Christ. Our communion with each other, and with the saints in heaven, is secondary to that. 'Primary' and 'secondary', however, suggest that the two are separable, when the situation is that Christian people have found them more like two sides of the one coin, or even two names for the same side. It is not open to us to follow Christ and ignore the others who try to follow him too. Here we approach the mysterious blurring of the distinction between the individual and the company which we find both in the Servant Songs in Isaiah and in the talk of Christ, the Spirit and the Church in the Gospels, especially that of John.

The second feature of the Church which is emphasised by the phrase 'Communion of Saints' is what we usually associate with the word 'saint'—the custom of regarding certain members of the Church as worthy of particular note as examples and guides in Christian discipleship. In the New Testament, it was acceptable to refer to all the members of a Christian congregation as saints, even in epistles which would later contain references to the same people demonstrating inclinations and habits which few would regard as saintly. The saintliness or holiness of these people lay not in their virtues, but in their sharing in the holiness of God, and that is always a fair way to think of the good qualities allegedly possessed by any of us. The same writers, however, were not slow to advocate desirable qualities of living and thinking, and the time soon came when individual members of the Church became the objects of great veneration for goodness and power over evil, both in their lifetime and after their death. We live in a different time, when popular versions of psychological studies and other factors lead us to look for skeletons in the cupboards of the great, and assume that there is badness in the best of us, and, possibly, goodness in the worst of us. In such an atmosphere, two things may help to build a bridge to (or from) the world of saints. One is the consideration that, whatever undesirable qualities individuals may have, there is great value in emphasising their good points, even as we accept that what count as good points will vary from place to place and from time to time, in the context of the Church as in society at large. The other thing is that Christian people have strong grounds in the Bible for seeking and recognising, not so much the good or saintly individual, as the good and saintly community.

The third feature of the Church appropriate to mention now is the sharing by Christian people in holy things, especially the Lord's Supper, where the height of our worship is expressed not in ideas or in feelings, but in doing things with things. 'Communion of Saints' in Latin is *Communio Sanctorum,* which can mean 'Communion of Holy Things' as well as 'Communion of Holy People'. The intimate relationship of the Church to the matter of the world serves to remind us of the connection of redemption to creation, and of the Church to the fulfilment of all things, all people, all life. The sheer puzzling mystery of the Communion of Saints should help us not to think of the Church of Jesus Christ as a human organisation.

15

The Forgiveness of Sins

A SCOTTISH preacher of the nineteenth century, expounding the Parable of the Prodigal Son, made this remark which is possibly as welcome for its frankness as it is sub-Christian in its content: 'If I had been that boy's father, I might have had him back, but I would not have held a party for him'. The divine grace which we affirm and celebrate in Christian believing is not a carefully calculated bowl of nourishment, sufficient for our needs but with not a spoonful extra. It is lavish, extravagant, unlimited generosity. That preacher would not have composed the line in Psalm 23: 'My cup runneth over'. I wonder what, if anything, went through his head when he sang it.

Some years ago, I visited a school and preached a sermon about the Parable of the Prodigal Son. Afterwards, a woman said to me that I ought to have told the young people that the Prodigal Son's father gave him a good scolding for being a bad boy. 'But that is not in the parable,' I said weakly, going on to try to suggest that it was also a fairly precise denial of the point of the parable. Undaunted, she told me that it was not right that my young hearers should get the impression that they could do all sorts of bad things and not be punished for them. Later in the conversation, she tackled me on the decision to install a window in St Giles' Cathedral in memory of the poet Robert Burns. A great poet he may have been, and the maker of lovely songs, but how on earth could I justify a tribute in a Christian Church to a man whose relationships with women were notoriously unchaste? As I prepared to murmur some placatory defence (it was late on Sunday evening and I didn't feel like an argument) her husband said quietly, 'The Prodigal Son?' 'Exactly,' said I, with relief.

If the subsequent parts of the Creed are an account of the meaning of the first part—'I believe in God ...'—the part we consider now could be described as a summary of that account. The phrase 'the forgiveness of sins' can be interpreted with fairness to the New Testament as meaning nothing less than the consequences of Christ's life, the whole scope of the benefit that is brought through him. It means much more than the assurance that God loves us despite the wrong we have done and the good we have left undone—unless that means simply that 'God loves us' is our expression of our knowledge that we have sensed our place in the universe and that it is a place of freedom and security and hope. Does that not indicate the essence of worship and the essence of living by the spirit of Christ?

One question at this point is, should we talk about sins or sin? When the prayer *Agnus Dei* is said in the Communion, it usually says 'Lamb of God, that takest away the sins of the world', a translation of the words familiar from classical masses: *Agnus Dei, qui tollis peccata mundi*. But these words come from the New Testament, where John the Baptist is quoted as saying 'Behold the lamb of God, which taketh away the sin of the world'. Every time I lead the Communion, I put 'sin' in the singular, not only in loyalty to the New Testament's text but, I hope, in loyalty to its spirit. Of course there is an understanding in the New Testament of sins as specific errors or omissions, but that understanding is part of a more fundamental thought about sin, or sinfulness, as the power of separation from God, the dynamic disposition to self-interest and self-indulgence, the pretence of self-sufficiency, and even a force which can be spoken of as you would speak of a person, such as the Devil or Satan. Through

Christian history both senses of sin have been present—the specific wrongs and the wider tendency. The forgiveness of sin, or of sins, refers to both together, and not to the forgiving of individual sins without the forgiving of sinfulness. The Gospel says more about the latter than the former, in the sense that we continue to sin, but the assurance of the overcoming of sinfulness, or Sin with a capital 'S', is given to us, and is not conditional on our being perfect in every detail. It is important to see that God's acceptance of us after we break the link with him by doing something wrong is not the whole story of his acceptance of us. The link is broken by pride and self-reliance in what we think of as good deeds, as well as in the things most people call sins. Alienation from God does not depend on wrongful activity.

Is there something unsatisfactory in the chief benefit of Christ being described as the sorting of something which has gone wrong? Could we not talk more positively about him? Certainly the note of a fundamental flaw in humanity has been sounded throughout Christian times, and preachers have echoed St Paul in saying that all have sinned and come short of the glory of God, quickly appending their own lists of sins, which vary greatly from time to time. We can try to speak as broadly and as uncensoriously about grace and new life as we may, and even talk about the reconciling purpose of Christ being not only the reconciliation of people with God, but their reconciliation with each other and the integrity of the whole universe, and quote such comprehensive thoughts as:

If any man be in Christ, he is a new creature: old thing are passed away; behold, all things are become new. And all things are of God, who hath reconciled us to himself by Jesus Christ, and have given to us the ministry of reconciliation; to wit, that God was in Christ, reconciling the world unto himself, not imputing their trespasses unto them; and hath committed unto us the word of reconciliation. Now then we are ambassadors for Christ, as though God did beseech you by us: we pray you in Christ's stead, be ye reconciled to God. For he hath made him to be sin for us, who knew no sin; that we might be made the righteousness of God in him.

Still does there not remain a regret that human nature is described by so many—and described with conviction and even relish—as fundamentally flawed? Can we not also see the grace which comes in Christ as encouragement of our essential goodness, as much as it is medicine for our essential sickness of the soul? To be incomplete is not a weakness, but the prerequisite of loving and being loved, and of growing and changing and living. I therefore think we might well try to read our references to forgiveness in a wider perspective than the overcoming of something that is wrong with us, and see forgiveness also as the acceptance and encouragement and friendship which make life liveable and bring to life its glory. Do you not even consider it possible that it is the spirit of Christ that inspires people to suspect an over-negative emphasis on sinfulness as unhealthy? Of course there is good and bad in all of us; but the distinction between the good and the bad is nothing near as easy to make, as censorious moralists of every generation suppose. Grace is capable of reflection in strange and shabby things, and goodness without grace can be terribly hard. To celebrate in worship a wholeness of life, and read that wholeness in terms of Jesus Christ, is as near a positive awareness of the forgiveness of sins and the nub of Christianity as I can imagine.

16

The Resurrection of the Body

I HAVE already tried to draw attention to the importance of regarding the phrases in the Creed as signposts which indicate—or even,
more modestly, suggest—the route by which Christian people
may travel together, exercising a deep trust and a lively hope in the
practice of life. It is not to be seen as a list of conclusions which
every person who says it has reached, as an expression of private
judgment or personal conviction.

There is, I suggest, at the present time a particular danger
involved in the widespread notion that being Christian involves,
supremely, personal beliefs and religious experience which take
precedence over the faith of the Church, which cannot in any
measure be a substitute for them—the danger being not only to the
spiritual and emotional and intellectual well-being of those who
think that way, but also to all the others who in earlier days would
be 'broad church people', but now may be inclined to regard
themselves debarred from belonging because they have insufficient
personal conviction or experience. The Church is and must be
filled with the whole mixture of types of attitude and understanding and emotion, and the faith proclaimed by the Church as
a whole will not represent the convinced judgment of any one
honest individual. Such an approach may seem to be too per-
missive an escape clause to be true; but I believe it is true.

I do not say that any opinions about anything are compatible
with Church membership; for a sense of attachment to the heart of
it all is essential. But how the details of that attachment are under-

stood must vary greatly, as the knowledge of the human race expands—and in some areas contracts—and as the experience and equipment of individual people vary from each other or within the lifetime of any person. These considerations will apply with much point to the last two phrases of the Creed, where knowledge of the physical world and the cultural perspective of our times make it hard to say with conviction that we believe in the resurrection of the body and the life everlasting. Not only that, but gentleness is required in talking of these areas which come so near to our fears and hopes about ourselves and the people who matter most to us, and many of us may wish to cling to what measure of belief we have about them not by spelling it out but by keeping as silent as possible about it.

Regarding them as to some extent one theme, I wish to say some things about the resurrection of the body and the life everlasting which seem to me to be helpful in our attempt not so much to think more clearly as to trust more practically in the deep areas of life and death which matter so much to us. Concerning the resurrection of the body, there are four points I wish to make now:

The first is that the emphasis on the body has particular importance for Christianity at any time, and added significance for the time in which the Creed was composed, when some were stressing their view that the body and all things physical were evil, with the Christian offer being one of salvation of the spirit by its rescue from the evil body. But the Church declared, and declares, that creation is good, that body and soul are inseparable, and that the offer of resurrection—whatever it is—is of a new life which combines in some way the spiritual and the physical as the life we have now combines them. St Paul speaks of our being given spiritual bodies, but cannot and does not say what that means. Perhaps what matters is that the emphasis is on the things which link us to other people—the senses—and that the new life offered is neither spiritual to the exclusion of physical, nor solitary to the exclusion of company.

The second thing to say is that what is meant by resurrection is directly linked to what is meant by Christ's resurrection, which in the New Testament is understood not as a demonstration of human achievement on the part of Christ but as an act of God. God raised Christ for us and offers us the same newness of life, not only when we die, but now. 'For as in Adam all die, even so in Christ shall all be made alive.'

The third thing is that baptism is offered as a sign of our sharing Christ's death and his new life.

Have you forgotten [St Paul wrote to the Romans] *that when we were baptised into union with Christ Jesus we were baptised into his death? By baptism we were buried with him and lay dead, in order that, as Christ was raised from the dead in the splendour of the Father, so also we might set our feet upon the new path of life. For if we have become incorporate with him in a death like his, we shall also be one with him in a resurrection like his.*

The fourth point is that the Holy Communion also brings together life and death and new life, our own as we share his. His brokenness and wholeness are offered to us together, and we receive his new life and the habit of giving up and receiving in newness more than we could begin to imagine or understand.

When Jesus is quoted in the St John's Gospel, chapter 3, as saying, 'You must be born again', was he advocating one singular event or experience, never to be repeated? Might he have been commending a lifelong disposition, a style of life, a perspective of detachment and involvement reminiscent of the Old

Testament prohibition of giving worship to idols? The value of material things lay in their not being treated as if they were God, just as his statement that 'the Sabbath was made for man, not man for the Sabbath' is a declaration that the Sabbath was a good thing—not, as may often be misunderstood, that he thought it was a bad thing. Without pressing the connection of being 'born again' to dying and rising with Christ (at least not in the sense of regarding birth as a form of death in the loss of the warm safety of the mother's womb, since even if that is valid it is somewhat confusing and disturbing to call birth 'death') I willingly suggest that there can be no separation in Christian believing of life beyond death from life here and now. What depth can there be to our hope if it is confined to heaven, and not expressed in attitudes and deeds of hope in relation to our fellows here on earth? What confidence can we have about death as the great 'change' if we treat the inevitable changes of life as if they threatened our heart and soul? Of course the loss of dear things can be painful, and the apparent detachment of a contrived stiff upper lip is completely different from a sensitive faith which feels the pain of many little deaths and yet knows that that is life.

17

And the Life everlasting

I HAVE given to these sermons on the Apostles' Creed the title of 'A Workable Belief?' because I wanted to encourage the thought that the Creed is of practical value—not a list of ideas to be cherished within the confines of detached exclusive religion, but indicators of a perspective on life with great significance for the way we regard our lives and the world around us, and for the priorities of behaviour and the style of relationships. The Christian importance of the forgiveness of sins, for example, lies not in the commendation of a gracious tolerance of other people (since there is nothing exclusively Christian about that) but in the practical consequences of our being accepted graciously by God (however we interpret that mysterious notion). The practical importance of these doctrinal signposts does not cease when we come to the last parts of the Creed.

A few years ago I met a Scot who lived in South Africa. He took me by surprise, in the middle of a general conversation, by asking, 'Do you believe Christ will come again?' I set out on a fairly rambling reply in which I suggested that it was not easy to discover what the writers of the New Testament thought about the subject; but he interrupted me to say that he believed the Lord would come again, and that when he came, he would lead black people and white people to live together as equals. 'I cannot see blacks and whites living together now,' he said, 'but when the Lord comes he will make it happen.' Was he using his belief in the second coming to excuse not doing anything to promote equality now? Or was he asserting the quality of the races while regretting its absence in practice? You can see how it was possible to employ the notion of a perfect order out in the afterworld either as a spur to move in that direction now, or as an excuse for doing nothing about moving in that direction.

Jesus made a positive connection between eternal life and present conduct when he was asked about gaining eternal life and told the parable of the good Samaritan. He also replied to the same question by telling the rich young man to give his wealth to the poor:

The Jesus beholding him loved him, and said unto him, One thing thou lackest: go thy way, sell whatever thou hast, and give to the poor, and thou shalt have treasure in heaven; and come, take up the cross, and follow me.

And he was sad at that saying, and went away grieved: for he had great possessions.

What is the connection between the above and the following saying of Jesus in St John's Gospel?

And this is life eternal, that they might know thee the only true God, and Jesus Christ, whom thou hast sent.

Is it not the freedom to trust, or the freedom to love, or the freedom from fear, which is both the knowledge of God and liberation from dependence on things? You might say that the whole purpose of religion is the encouragement of that freedom to live in trust and hope.

It must be clear that whatever eternal or everlasting life is, it is not something which begins when we die, but something which we are offered now. It is true that much has been written suggesting the character of the glorious existence which lies ahead of us beyond this earthly life; but like my friend from South Africa talking about race relations, people can use their fine descriptions of glory in two opposite ways. By noting the things that are wrong in their present life they can paint a picture of the life hereafter as a life where all their negatives are replaced by positives —and that can have the effect of running away from the present and living only in a world of dreams. In some circumstances that is perfectly understandable, as when slaves sang of the heaven in which they would be free. Yet Jesus offered freedom now, and the option lies available of building such dreams as we have, not upon the negation of the wrong things now, but upon the confirmation of the right things now, in such a way as gives us greater appreciation of what is good here and now, and greater desire to seek the increase of what is good here and now. The way that Jesus spoke of eternal life in the verses I have quoted, more than suggests that he advocated a way of thinking and living which overcame the fear of death, not as if it were the only thing to fear, but because the overcoming of that particular fear was included in the overcoming of fear in general, which is more positively described as the adoption of hope and trust.

The making of detailed descriptions of heaven is riddled with hazard. Do you find the idea of peace forever appealing? Only if the peace is defined in the right way, don't you think? Do you find the idea of life where all is sunshine without clouds appealing? What do you make of the notion of a perpetual banquet, or an interminable harp concert, or a world of smiling chumminess? The fact is that we would want different sorts of heaven, and we should not take these poetic images too seriously. Perhaps more helpful is St Paul's saying, in his great chapter about charity:

For now we see through a glass, darkly; but then face to face: now I know in part; but then shall I know even as also I am known.

You find there three ideas which seem to me to be helpful—first, that we have only the odd glimpse of the truth of the mysteries of life; second, that eternal life consists in our nearness to God; and third, that in this life our nearness to God depends more on his knowledge of us than on our knowledge of him.

Thus the end of the Creed speaks to us as did the beginning—of belief in the God and Father of Our Lord Jesus Christ; that is, it speaks to us of a basic trust and hope in living, kindled and encouraged by the things of Christ in scriptures, Church and sacrament, and in every true experience of life's mysteries, of nature's wonders.

18

Not the Last Word

WHAT are we to make of the Apostles' Creed? Jesus' statement that the Sabbath was made for man, not man for the Sabbath, may serve as a useful clue. The Creed is there to serve our interest, rather than our liberty and peace being crammed and twisted into what some might regard as the doctrinal straightjacket of the Creed. A taxi-driver in Paisley was asked by a newspaper reporter to give his opinion of relationships between Catholics and Protestants in that town, and he replied, 'Religion is fine, so long as you don't make a God of it'. Quite so. We should not forget that 'religion' includes statements, definitions, and vocabulary about God. The word 'God' is fine, so long as you do not deify it. The Creed is not the last word about anything. 'For now we see through a glass, darkly, but then face to face.' Only then. Such an approach does not diminish the significance of it, but rather enhances it. 'We have this treasure in earthen vessels, that the excellency of the power may be of God, and not of us.'

In the Acts of the Apostles we read about Peter having a strange dream in which he was offered animals which Jews were forbidden to eat, and a voice from heaven telling him that 'What God hath cleansed, that call not thou common'. When he woke he was invited to go and welcome a man who was not Jewish into the Christian Church. Peter put the vision into practice, and the man was indeed welcomed. The Church leaders in Jerusalem were troubled, and challenged Peter about the incident; but when they had heard him, they changed their minds about keeping Gentiles out of the Church, and concluded that 'then hath God also the Gentiles granted repentance unto life'. The order of events is deeply significant: first, the dream or vision or insight or spiritual experience; then, the practice of the insight; and only after that, the alteration of doctrine to take account of the new situation. It seems sadly common for people to assume another order—first, getting your doctrine or beliefs sorted out, and only then seeking to express them in worship and daily living. Theology is the hand-maid of worship and practice, not their heart and soul. Things like Creeds can help us on our journey of experience in which things of the spirit and things of the body and the community are intertwined; but things like Creeds should not be used as obstacles to that journey.

Do you not gather from the Gospels that Jesus was not much given to pronouncing the last word? Instead of issuing doctrinal pronouncements, he shared with his hearers epigrams, stories, pregnant and elusive utterances, which through all these centuries have puzzled people into fresh thinking and new interpretation across the constantly changing environments of the developing world. He is reported as saying both that he was the light of the world and that his hearers were the light of the world, both that those who were not with him were against him and also that those who were not against him were on his side (and the more frequent quoting of the exclusive version testifies to the inclination of a certain sort of 'religious' person in the direction of exclusive-ness rather than inclusiveness).

One of Jesus' central themes—perhaps his one central theme —was that of the Kingdom of God, the further definition of which has exercised mighty minds ever since. (There is no basis in the New Testament for the view of Jesus which regards him as a smiling cherub going around with nothing more verbose than 'Love' on his lips.) If we agree with most of the Church that the aim, vision, or ideal in the idea of the Kingdom included the element of universal peace and the fulfilment and perfection of all nature, it follows that we will not regard the Church as an end in itself, or its component instruments as ultimate or fundamental. The question, Does the peace of the world matter deeply to Christian faith?, does not arise. What does arise is the question, How far does Christian faith as we understand and practise it help or hinder the peace of the world?

I reckon that there are many people who deeply desire the peace of the world and their own personal peace, and who regard the two as interdependent. The prophet Jeremiah made that point when he advised the exiled Jews in Babylon to settle down, cultivate their gardens, encourage intermarriage, and seek the peace of the city of Babylon, 'for in the peace thereof shall ye find peace'. What many in our time must find hard to accept is the value of doctrinal points such as the ingredients of the Creed in the search for either individual or universal peace. The puzzle and the doubt are understandable, and Christian preachers must listen long and carefully to the exponents of such attitudes. What cannot be doubted is that over the past century the human race has learned much about the immense complexities of our personalities, the intricate connection of inheritance and past experience to present health of mind and body, and the naive inappropriateness of supposing that problems in human affairs could be solved by sensible attitudes displayed by reasonable people. We are only partly creatures of reason. The factors which shape our dispositions and form our reactions are deep and mysterious. It is no mark of the unsuitability of Christian signs and symbols to say that they are complicated and deep.

Perhaps it is in the Holy Communion, the Lord's Supper, the Eucharist, the Mass, that complexity and simplicity come most creatively together for Christian people. There we become the

Church in a way we are not at other times. (We are always more or less the Church, never totally and fully so.) There the stuff of earth and the rumours of heaven intermingle, and the things of Christ provide the perspective by which to look at all life, and to see ourselves and others in the light of hope and trust and love.